Memories: Vintage Cake Recipes

Copyright © 2013 by Becky Johnson

Published by Cool Things Press

www.coolthingspress.com

ISBN: 978-0615781761

Memories

Vintage Cake Recipes

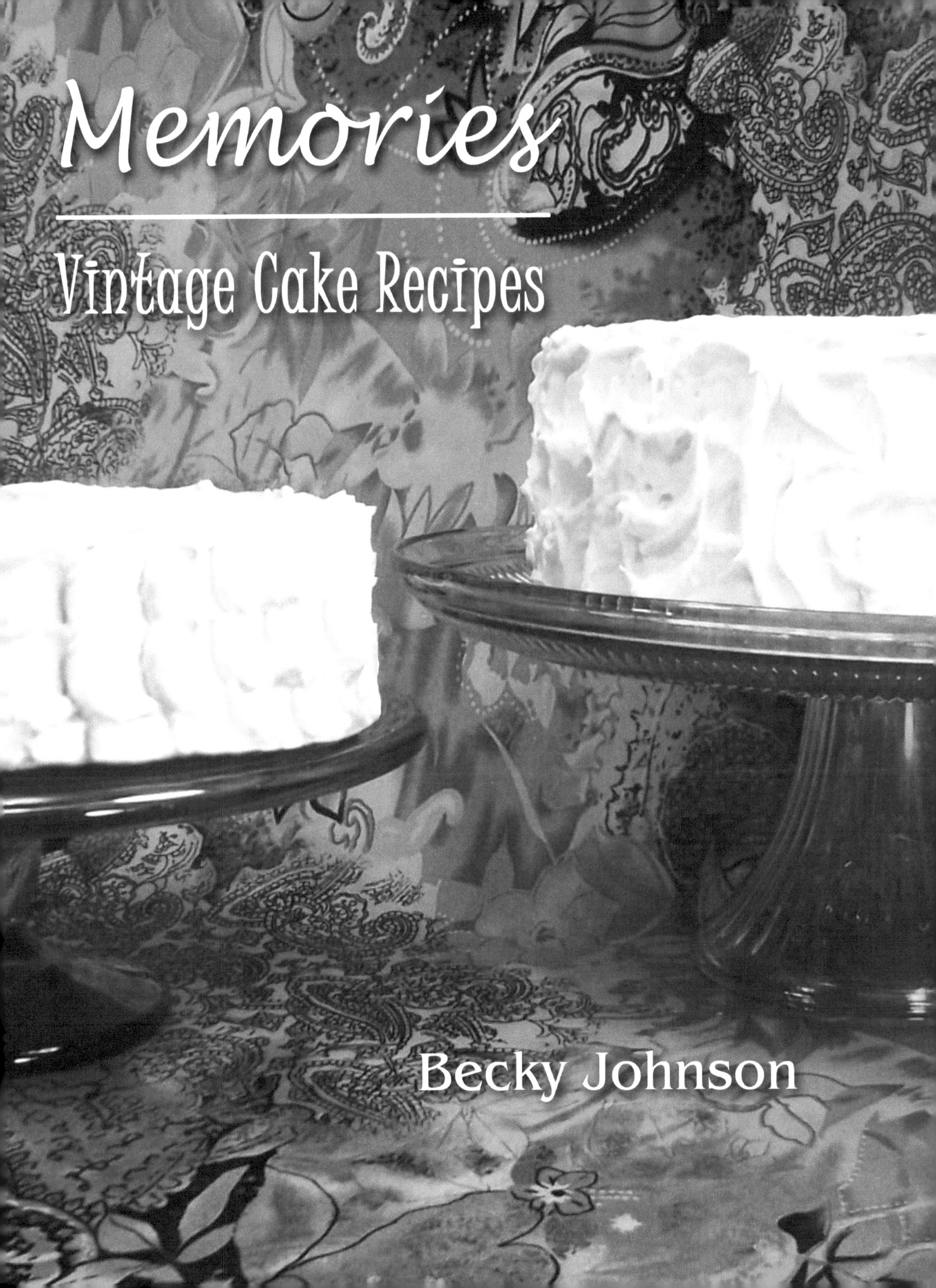

Becky Johnson

CONTENTS

CONTENTS

INTRODUCTION

In recent years, there has been renewed interest in all things retro. Perhaps it is because technology propels us forward at such a swift rate, that we all long to reach back for something from our past for comfort and security.

Recipes, like technology, have had their own evolution, although the progression hasn't been quite so hasty. Like the slow pace of waiting for a loaf of bread to rise, recipes have evolved over the centuries from handed down concoctions to handwritten cards to magazine clippings. Ingredients have changed with the help of technology, mass production and agriculture. Home baking as it was in the old days would now be considered a health threat with all the worries about carbs, butter and sugar. Nowadays, (assuming the adventurous home cook doesn't want boxed cake mix or a frozen meal), instead of those magazine clippings, you'll find the latest handheld computerized device propped up against the flour jar, recipe gleaming brightly on its display, waiting to be attempted.

Today's recipes are more complex than their predecessors, likely due to our more complex palettes and health consciousness. Gone are the days of the short and sweet recipe—they've been replaced by more complicated works of television chefs and health gurus. In my treasure trove of old recipes, I found a note card that included a short list of ingredients, which included a pound of butter, and a brief set of steps that said, "...mix like you would any other cake..." and, "cook in a slow oven until done..." Not really the greatest instructions for an intermediate home cook, and even more of a challenge for a novice who just wants a taste of what Grandma might have baked but doesn't have any "baking intuition" or advanced skills.

My ethnic background is a diverse mix of regional and international influences. My mother was from Louisiana, born in the 1920s with Scottish-German ancestry. She grew up in a large, poor family on a rural farm. They used fresh ingredients that they grew themselves, and they baked on a daily basis. My father's parents immigrated to America from Italy and Spain in the 1920s. They made and sold ethnic foods, and in their broken English, imparted their recipes and techniques to my Mother when she married my father. I was the last of seven kids in a middle-class California household surrounded by good food and lots of family. I spent time in the Pacific Northwest, and I now live in New England, and I find that my husband's familial "wicked nor'easter" influences creep into my cooking every now and then.

When I was a child, I was always at my mother's side when she was in the kitchen. I savored her cooking, all the way up until she died in 2002. Each time I bake, I think of her. Lately, my daughters have developed a strong interest in baking and I try my best to share what I know with them. It's my duty and pleasure as their mother to help them know their ancestors, even though they never had the opportunity to meet.

My profession is technology, but I love home baking. The idea for this book came about because one of my daughters was having a birthday party and I wanted to create a special cake. I found an archive box of my mother's cake recipes and started reminiscing. I found a cake recipe for the birthday party, but as I was reading Mom's calligraphic scrawl while trying to decipher the meaning of slow and moderate ovens, I felt like I could pay homage to my mother and my ancestors if I shared some of their heirloom recipes. Call it perpetuating a lost art, but I felt it was important to deliver the recipes as they were meant to be baked. They haven't been "healthified" or "improved" and they're just as sweet as originally prescribed.

Baking—especially cake baking—is chemistry, alchemy, art and intuition. Be patient and persistent when you take on any recipe. Think about the ingredients and ways you might try to improve or improvise, and suit the recipe to your own taste. Our ancestors did not always use by-the-book measurements. A cup here and a dash there always seemed to turn out right, which seems like magic if you struggle with six-ounce cups versus eight-ounce cups and how to level dry ingredients properly! Aside of understanding terminology in vintage recipes, one of the challenges is finding ingredients. In case you don't use mace or citron in everyday dishes, I've listed some suppliers I used to find these gems, and the results were worth the hunt.

This compilation was tested in my kitchen, using basic everyday tools. All measures, baking temperatures and times have been verified. Many of these recipes have been extrapolated from brief notes—some had no specific directions. Each recipe has its own history, and each region and culture has their own versions of the same recipes, so you may recognize many in this collection.

Additionally, I include in this book notes from my mother's and grandmother's cooking journal. My mother was fortunate enough to have inherited her own mother's sagacity in well-kept annotated order, and I have inherited the same. You will also find some glaze, frosting and icing recipes which may be used interchangeably on the cakes.

I hope that this collection will evoke good memories for you as it has for me, and maybe even create some new memories.

— Becky Johnson

Notes from Mom & Grandma

❀ Read through a recipe in its entirety before beginning. Make sure you have all ingredients at room temperature, pre-measured if possible, and that your pans are prepared accordingly.

❀ Always use stainless steel or copper mixing bowls for beating egg whites. Plastic will greatly delay production of stiff whites.

❀ When beating whipping cream, always be sure that everything is chilled and perfectly clean, including your tools and bowls.

❀ To grease and flour pans means to coat them thoroughly, including corners, first with fat, such as butter, shortening or lard, and then dust them lightly with flour. Tap out any excess flour.

❀ Baking paper is the equivalent of modern day parchment paper. For the best results when baking cakes, always line the bottom only of the pan with baking paper unless the recipe states otherwise.

❀ Always preheat oven and place the rack in the center unless the recipe states otherwise. Be sure your oven is level; otherwise your cakes will be uneven.

❀ When selecting mixing bowls, always have available several sizes to accommodate your ingredients. It is better to work in a bowl that is a little too large than to have to transfer batter into a new bowl if you've made a mistake.

❀ Fill a cake pan no more and two-thirds full and evenly distribute batter out to all edges of the pan.

❀ Baking times will vary depending on the pan used. If a recipe calls for an 8" round and you use a larger pan, expect it to take less time because the cake will be thinner.

❀ If dark pans are used when baking a cake, the crust will be darker than if light pans are used. Glass baking dishes will also affect the color of the crust.

❀ When you mix together dry and liquid ingredients, do not allow them to sit; place in oven immediately.

❀ When mixing cake batter, never over mix. Only stir enough to incorporate ingredients unless the recipe states otherwise.

❀ In a pinch, to make cake flour, substitute 10-12% cornstarch for all-purpose flour and sift five times. For example, if your recipe calls for two cups of cake flour, measure two cups of all-purpose flour and remove one quarter cup then replace it with one quarter cup cornstarch.

❀ For best mixing results, unless a recipe specifies otherwise, cream sugar with fat first, and then add eggs. To avoid lumps, always add sifted dry ingredients alternately, a third at a time, with liquid ingredients. If a recipe calls for stiff egg whites, fold them into the batter last.

❀ Measure liquid ingredients in glass measuring cups on a level surface — liquid measures are not for dry ingredients.

❀ Measure dry ingredients in metal or plastic measuring cups and level the top with the flat edge of a knife.

❀ When measuring brown sugar, always pack it down into the measuring cup to get an accurate measurement unless the recipe states otherwise.

❀ Use salted butter unless the recipe specifically calls for unsalted butter. Most butter of the past was preserved using salt.

❀ Use whole milk unless the recipe states differently. Lower fat milk did not become popular until after World War II.

❀ When beating egg yolks and sugar, be sure to mix swiftly and do not allow them to sit without mixing. The sugar will "burn" the yolks, leaving hard bits that will ruin your cake.

❀ Use double-acting baking powder for cakes. Double-acting baking powder helps cakes to rise once cake batter is placed in a hot oven. Single-acting baking powder reacts to liquid ingredients right away, so if you don't get your cake in the oven immediately, the gases formed by the chemical reaction of the powder with liquids will escape and your cake won't rise as high, and may fall flat.

❀ Oleo was another name for margarine, sometimes butter. Saleratus was another name for baking soda. Homogenized Spry was a brand of shortening that was made in the mid-1930s until the 1960s. Cottolene was a brand of shortening made of beef tallow and cottonseed oil produced starting in the late 1860s as an alternative to lard.

❀ Always check the top of cake for firmness just before it is due to come out of the oven to avoid over cooking. You can also use a toothpick to check doneness.

❀ To stir means to mix all ingredients together with a utensil, usually a spoon, using a circular motion to integrate.

❀ To beat means all ingredients are stirred vigorously, sometimes using a balloon whisk or electric mixer.

❀ To cream ingredients means that fat and sugar are beaten together until they are light and airy in texture.

❀ To fold means that one ingredient is gently incorporated into another by hand with a large spoon or rubber spatula. Gently scoop ingredients from bottom of the bowl to top of batter while turning bowl slowly.

❀ Tempering means to elevate the temperature of an ingredient by adding slowly small amounts of a hot or boiling liquid. Tempering helps to avoid curdling ingredients such as eggs.

❀ Beat egg whites using a stand mixer, hand mixer or balloon whisk. Begin by beating slowly until large air bubbles form, then increase speed to medium. Foam will increase and become white. Increase speed to high and beat until egg whites reach the soft peak stage (whites will droop when whisk is lifted). Continue to beat until the whites are fluffy, firm and glossy. Do not over beat as egg whites will become dry and unusable.

Black Walnut Tea Cake

Tea cake has evolved from bun-like yeast biscuits which contained dried fruit and nuts, to the spice cake we know it as today. This recipe is a variant from the 1920s and uses fresh black walnuts and brown sugar to make a sweet and crunchy topping.

❧ Preheat oven to 350 degrees. Grease and flour one 9" x 9" x 2" cake pan. Line bottom with parchment paper.

1. In a mixing bowl, cream together butter and 1 cup of the brown sugar.
2. Add corn syrup and vanilla extract.
3. Beat in eggs, one at a time.
4. In a separate bowl, mix and sift together flour, baking powder and salt, then add to creamed mixture alternately with milk.
5. Pour into cake pan and sprinkle with mixture of walnuts and remaining brown sugar. Pat in lightly.
6. Bake for 40 minutes or until toothpick inserted comes out clean.

Ingredients

- ◆ 1/2 CUP BUTTER
- ◆ 1 CUP LIGHT BROWN SUGAR
- ◆ 3/4 CUP WHITE CORN SYRUP
- ◆ 2 TEASPOONS VANILLA EXTRACT
- ◆ 4 EGGS
- ◆ 2 1/2 CUPS CAKE FLOUR
- ◆ 3 TEASPOONS BAKING POWDER
- ◆ 1/4 TEASPOON SALT
- ◆ 1/2 CUP MILK

TOPPING:

- ◆ 1/2 CUP BLACK WALNUTS, CHOPPED
- ◆ 1/2 CUP LIGHT BROWN SUGAR

Bride's Cake

In contrast to the contemporary wedding cake's austerity, this cake used to be broken over the top of a bride's head, and stood for symbolism of fertility and rite of passage. This cake has a soft but dense crumb, and works well with American Buttercream Frosting or Vanilla Glaze, page 66.

❧ Preheat oven to 325 degrees. Grease and flour one 10" tube pan.

1. In a metal mixing bowl, beat egg whites until stiff; set aside.
2. In a another bowl, cream together butter and sugar until fluffy.
3. Separately, mix and sift together flour, cream of tartar, and baking soda, then add to creamed mixture alternately with milk.
4. Fold in beaten egg whites and almond extract.
5. Bake for 50 minutes or until toothpick inserted comes out clean.

Ingredients

- ◆ 8 EGG WHITES
- ◆ 1 CUP BUTTER
- ◆ 2 CUPS GRANULATED SUGAR
- ◆ 3 CUPS ALL-PURPOSE FLOUR
- ◆ 1 TEASPOON CREAM OF TARTAR
- ◆ 1/2 TEASPOON BAKING SODA
- ◆ 1/2 CUP MILK
- ◆ 1/2 TEASPOON ALMOND EXTRACT

Black Walnut Tea Cake

Bride's Cake, shown with American Buttercream Frosting, page 66

Cream Cake

This simple and quick cake is a variation of the Snow Cake and uses thin cream, which would be the modern day equivalent of half and half. Cream Cake is light and fluffy with a soft crumb and will work with most flavors of frosting.

❧ Preheat oven to 325 degrees. Grease and flour one 8" x 2" round cake pan. Line bottom with parchment paper.

1. In a mixing bowl, beat together eggs, sugar, vanilla extract and cream.
2. In another bowl, mix and sift together flour, baking powder and salt and add to creamed mixture.
3. Pour batter into cake pan and bake for 30 minutes or until toothpick inserted comes out clean.

Ingredients

- 2 EGGS
- 7/8 CUP GRANULATED SUGAR
- 1 TEASPOON VANILLA EXTRACT
- 2/3 CUP THIN CREAM
- 1 2/3 CUPS ALL-PURPOSE FLOUR
- 2 1/2 TEASPOONS BAKING POWDER
- 1/2 TEASPOON SALT

Creole Beauty Cake

From 1930s New Orleans, this tall stacked cake with cherries and nuts in each bite was baked to impress. Bake this cake using three equal-size 8" rounds, or substitute one for a smaller 6" round at the top, as shown.

❧ Preheat oven to 350 degrees. Grease and flour three 8" x 2" round cake pans. Line bottoms with parchment paper.

1. In a bowl, combine shortening and almond extract.
2. Add sugar and cream together well.
3. In another bowl, mix and sift together flour, salt and baking powder and add to creamed mixture alternately with milk.
4. In a metal mixing bowl, beat egg whites until stiff, then fold into batter.
5. To 2/3 of batter, add food coloring and almonds, and then pour into two of the cake pans.
6. To remaining batter add cherries, and then pour into third cake pan.
7. Bake for 30 minutes. Cool completely.
8. When assembling, alternate layers, starting with one of the red layers, then the white layer, and then red.

Ingredients

- 2/3 CUP SHORTENING
- 1 TEASPOON ALMOND EXTRACT
- 1 1/2 CUPS GRANULATED SUGAR
- 3 CUPS CAKE FLOUR
- 3/4 TEASPOON SALT
- 3 1/2 TEASPOONS BAKING POWDER
- 1 CUP MILK
- 4 EGG WHITES
- 1 TEASPOON RED FOOD COLORING
- 3/4 CUP ALMONDS, CHOPPED
- 1/2 CUP MARASCHINO CHERRIES, CHOPPED

Cream Cake, shown with Marshmallow Frosting, page 68

Creole Beauty Cake, shown with a cherry, almonds and American Buttercream Frosting, page 66

Chocolate Cake

Originally reserved for religious ceremonies due to its expense, when the price of chocolate dropped after World War I, chocolate desserts became popular. Use milk or coffee in this cake. Milk will allow for a soft crumb while coffee will make the flavor of the chocolate bolder.

Preheat oven to 350 degrees. Grease and flour one 9" x 9" x 2" cake pan. Line bottom with parchment paper.

1. In a mixing bowl, cream together butter and sugar, gradually adding in melted chocolate and vanilla extract. Add egg yolks.
2. In a separate mixing bowl, mix and sift together flour, baking powder and salt, then add alternately with milk (or coffee) to creamed mixture.
3. Pour batter into cake pan and bake for 40 minutes or until top is firm to touch.

Ingredients

- 1/2 CUP BUTTER
- 1 1/4 CUPS GRANULATED SUGAR
- 3 OUNCES BITTERSWEET CHOCOLATE, 60% CACAO, MELTED
- 1/2 TEASPOON VANILLA EXTRACT
- 2 EGG YOLKS, BEATEN
- 2 CUPS ALL-PURPOSE FLOUR
- 2 TEASPOONS BAKING POWDER
- 1/2 TEASPOON SALT
- 1 CUP MILK OR COFFEE, BREWED STRONG

Chiffon Cake

In the 1920s, Harry Baker, a Los Angeles insurance salesman, supposedly developed this cake wherein salad oil is substituted for butter. During the 1940s through the 1960s, just about every women's magazine published some variation of this recipe.

Preheat oven to 325 degrees. Grease and flour one 10" tube pan.

1. In a metal mixing bowl, beat egg whites until fluffy.
2. Add cream of tartar and continue beating until stiff; set aside.
3. In a separate bowl, mix and sift together flour, sugar, baking powder and salt. Make a well in the dry ingredients to hold liquid ingredients.
4. Add oil, egg yolks, water, lemon juice and vanilla extract. Beat until smooth. Gently fold in egg whites.
5. Pour batter into cake pan. Bake for 45 minutes.
6. Remove from oven and invert pan and allow to hang free until cooled. To remove, loosen with a spatula.

Ingredients

- 4 EGGS, SEPARATED
- 1/4 TEASPOON CREAM OF TARTAR
- 1 1/8 CUPS ALL-PURPOSE FLOUR
- 3/4 CUP GRANULATED SUGAR
- 1 1/2 TEASPOONS BAKING POWDER
- 1/2 TEASPOON SALT
- 1/4 CUP VEGETABLE OIL
- 1/4 CUP WATER
- 1/2 TEASPOON LEMON JUICE
- 1/2 TEASPOON VANILLA EXTRACT

*Chocolate Cake,
shown with
Chocolate Fudge
Frosting, page 66*

*Chiffon Cake,
shown with
Marshmallow
Frosting, page 68*

Prize Cake, a.k.a. "Lane Cake"

This cake originated in 1898. Emma Rylander Lane one a prize for her recipe in a state fair, when it was called "Prize" Cake. The recipe has varied over time, especially the filling, but it has remained a favorite at holiday time in the Southern US. Add or subtract nuts and fruit to your taste.

❁ Preheat oven to 325 degrees. Grease and flour four 8" x 2" round cake pans. Line bottoms with parchment paper.

For the Cake:

1. In a mixing bowl, cream together butter and sugar.
2. In a separate bowl, mix and sift together flour, cream of tartar, baking powder, baking soda and salt, then add to the creamed mixture alternately with heavy cream.
3. Stir in vanilla extract.
4. Fold in the stiff egg whites.
5. Divide and pour batter into cake pans and bake for 25 minutes. Cool completely.

For the Filling:

1. In a saucepan on stove, heat egg yolks over medium heat for 1 minute.
2. Beat in sugar and melted butter. Cook for about 8 minutes, stirring constantly, until thick enough to coat back of spoon.
3. Remove from heat and stir in bourbon and vanilla extract, then add and stir in coconut, cherries, apricots, raisins, pecans and almonds.

To Assemble:

Divide filling into thirds and spread between layers of cake. For the top layer of the cake, frost with plain vanilla frosting, such as American Buttercream Frosting or Cooked Vanilla Icing.

Ingredients

CAKE:

- 1 CUP BUTTER, SOFTENED
- 2 CUPS GRANULATED SUGAR
- 3 1/4 CUPS CAKE FLOUR, SIFTED
- 2 TEASPOONS CREAM OF TARTAR
- 2 TEASPOONS BAKING POWDER
- 1 TEASPOON BAKING SODA
- 1/4 TEASPOON SALT
- 1 CUP HEAVY CREAM
- 2 TEASPOONS VANILLA EXTRACT
- 8 EGG WHITES, BEATEN TO STIFF PEAKS

FILLING:

- 8 EGG YOLKS, BEATEN
- 1 CUP GRANULATED SUGAR
- 8 TABLESPOONS BUTTER, MELTED AND COOLED
- 1/3 CUP BOURBON
- 1 TEASPOON VANILLA EXTRACT
- 1/2 CUP SHREDDED COCONUT, SWEETENED AND TOASTED
- 1/2 CUP CHERRIES, DRIED AND CHOPPED
- 1/2 CUP APRICOTS, DRIED AND CHOPPED
- 1/2 CUP RAISINS, CHOPPED
- 1/2 CUP PECANS, CHOPPED
- 1/2 CUP ALMONDS, TOASTED AND CHOPPED

Prize Cake, shown with American Buttercream Frosting, page 66

Pineapple Upside Down Cake

This cake became popular in the early 1900s when pineapple and maraschino cherries were easier to obtain. The idea of a one-pan cake that didn't need frosting was appealing to homemakers of the era. You can also use crushed pineapple and sneak in a little bit of the pineapple juice into the batter in place of some of the milk.

❦ Preheat oven to 350 degrees. Butter the sides and bottom of one 8" cast iron skillet.

1. Sprinkle brown sugar in bottom of cast-iron skillet. Dot with butter.
2. Melt mixture over very low heat on stove, and then remove from heat. Pat dry pineapple slices and arrange in bottom of pan. Add a cherry to the center of each. Set aside.
3. In a mixing bowl, mix and sift together flour, baking powder and salt.
4. In a separate bowl, cream together shortening and sugar, and gradually add egg and vanilla extract. Add flour mixture alternately with milk.
5. Pour batter over fruit. Bake for 50 minutes or until golden brown. Remove from oven and turn upside down onto serving plate immediately.

Ingredients

- 1/2 CUP LIGHT BROWN SUGAR
- 3 TABLESPOONS BUTTER
- 7-9 RINGS FRESH PEELED PINEAPPLE
- 7-9 MARASCHINO CHERRIES
- 2 CUPS CAKE FLOUR, SIFTED
- 3 TEASPOONS BAKING POWDER
- 1/4 TEASPOON SALT
- 1/4 CUP SHORTENING
- 1 CUP GRANULATED SUGAR
- 1 EGG
- 1 TEASPOON VANILLA EXTRACT
- 3/4 CUP MILK

Poppy Seed Cake

According to Strawbery Banke Museum in Portsmouth, New Hampshire, Jewish immigrants brought poppy seeds with them to America in the early 1900s, with which created delicious pastries. This sweet cake has a satisfying crunch in each bite.

❦ Preheat oven to 350 degrees. Grease and flour one 10" tube pan.

1. Soak poppy seeds in milk in a cup and set aside.
2. In a metal mixing bowl, beat egg whites until stiff and while beating, add 1/2 of the sugar in small increments, then set aside.
3. In a separate bowl, cream together shortening and vanilla extract. Add remaining sugar.
4. Separately, mix and sift together flour, salt and baking powder.
5. Add dry ingredients to creamed mixture, along with poppy seeds and milk. Batter will be thick.
6. Fold in beaten egg whites and sugar mixture.
7. Pour batter into cake pan and bake for 40 minutes.

Ingredients

- 1/2 CUP POPPY SEEDS
- 1 CUP MILK
- 4 EGG WHITES
- 1 1/2 CUPS GRANULATED SUGAR
- 1/2 CUP SHORTENING
- 2 TEASPOONS VANILLA EXTRACT
- 2 CUPS ALL-PURPOSE FLOUR
- 1 TEASPOON SALT
- 2 TEASPOONS BAKING POWDER

*Pineapple Upside
Down Cake*

Poppy Seed Cake

Carrot Cake

There is some documentation that indicates modern Carrot Cake arose from carrot pudding which was popular between the Middle Ages to the late 1700s. Like the Chiffon Cake, this cake is made with oil instead of butter. It has a large but soft crumb and crunchy sweet top, and is well-paired with Cream Cheese Frosting, page 68.

Preheat oven to 350 degrees. Grease and flour one 9" x 13" x 2" cake pan. Line bottom with parchment paper.

1. In a mixing bowl, beat together sugar and vegetable oil.
2. Add eggs and beat well.
3. In a separate bowl, mix and sift together flour, baking soda, cinnamon, and salt then add to eggs and oil mixture and beat well.
4. Add carrots, nuts, and then coconut, pineapple or raisins if desired.
5. Pour batter into cake pan and bake for 45 minutes.

Ingredients

- 2 CUPS GRANULATED SUGAR
- 1 1/4 CUPS VEGETABLE OIL
- 4 LARGE EGGS
- 2 CUPS ALL-PURPOSE FLOUR
- 2 TEASPOONS BAKING SODA
- 1 TABLESPOON CINNAMON
- 1 TEASPOON SALT
- 3 CUPS CARROTS, FINELY GRATED
- 1 CUP CHOPPED WALNUTS
- 1/4 CUP COCONUT, PINEAPPLE AND/OR RAISINS IF DESIRED

Ginger Cake

This recipe is a variant of traditional Gingerbread. Made with fresh ginger root, this cake is light, spongy and golden in contrast to its darker cousin. Be sure to mince the ginger root finely and drain off any liquid before using.

Preheat oven to 325 degrees. Grease and flour one 9" x 9" x 2" cake pan. Line bottom with parchment paper.

1. In a mixing bowl, cream together butter and sugar.
2. Add eggs and beat well.
3. In a separate mixing bowl, mix and sift together flour, baking powder and salt, then add to creamed mixture, alternating with milk.
4. Add ginger to batter and mix well.
5. Pour batter into pan and bake for 30 minutes or until top is firm to touch.

Ingredients

- 1/2 CUP BUTTER
- 1/2 CUP GRANULATED SUGAR
- 2 EGGS
- 1 1/4 CUPS ALL-PURPOSE FLOUR
- 1 TEASPOON BAKING POWDER
- 1/2 TEASPOON SALT
- 1/2 CUP MILK
- 1/2 CUP GINGER, FRESH, FINELY GRATED, CHOPPED AND DREDGED IN FLOUR

Carrot Cake

Ginger Cake, shown topped with Fresh Whipped Cream, page 70

Devil's Food Cake

The early 1900s answer to Angel Food Cake was a rich, decadent, "sinful" cake. Everything from milk to mashed potatoes has been used to create this soft-crumbed delight. The difference between simple Chocolate Cake and Devil's Food Cake is the amount and type of chocolate used. Use dark chocolate for a richer cake.

❧ Preheat oven to 350 degrees. Grease and flour one 10" tube pan.

1. In a mixing bowl, cream together butter and sugar.
2. Gradually add egg yolks; beat well.
3. In a separate mixing bowl, mix and sift together flour, cocoa powder, baking powder, baking soda and salt, then add alternately with milk to creamed mixture.
4. In a saucepan on stove, melt together chocolate, vanilla extract and coffee, then add to batter.
5. In a metal mixing bowl, beat egg whites until stiff and fold into batter.
6. Pour into tube pan and bake for 45 minutes or until a toothpick inserted comes out clean.

Ingredients

- ◆ 1/2 CUP BUTTER
- ◆ 2 CUPS GRANULATED SUGAR
- ◆ 4 EGGS, SEPARATED
- ◆ 2 1/2 CUPS CAKE FLOUR
- ◆ 1/4 CUP UNSWEETENED NATURAL COCOA POWDER
- ◆ 4 TEASPOONS BAKING POWDER
- ◆ 1/2 TEASPOON BAKING SODA
- ◆ 1/4 TEASPOON SALT
- ◆ 1 CUP MILK
- ◆ 4 OUNCES UNSWEETENED CHOCOLATE
- ◆ 1 TEASPOON VANILLA EXTRACT
- ◆ 1 TABLESPOON COFFEE, BREWED STRONG

Lemon Jelly Roll Cake

This cake can be challenging for the beginner, but it's an impressive feat once it's assembled. Use any fruit jam, compote or creamy custard as a filling. A level stove is important so that the cake cooks evenly.

❧ Preheat oven to 400 degrees. Grease one 15" x 10" x 1-1/2" cookie sheet. Line bottom with parchment paper.

1. In a mixing bowl, mix and sift together flour, salt and baking powder.
2. In another mixing bowl, cream together sugar, lemon extract and eggs, and then add sifted dry ingredients.
3. Pour batter evenly into pan and bake for 13 minutes; turn pan around after 7 minutes to ensure even baking.
4. Remove cake from oven. Trim edges if necessary.
5. Immediately spread jam out to edges of cake.
6. Working quickly, roll cake firmly, peeling away paper as you go; cake will be hot.

Ingredients

- ◆ 3/4 CUP CAKE FLOUR
- ◆ 1/4 TEASPOON SALT
- ◆ 1 TEASPOON BAKING POWDER
- ◆ 3/4 CUP GRANULATED SUGAR
- ◆ 1 TEASPOON LEMON EXTRACT
- ◆ 4 EGGS
- ◆ 1 CUP FRUIT JELLY OR JAM, SUCH AS LEMON OR BERRY, THICK CUSTARD OR COMPOTE

Devil's Food Cake, shown with Chocolate Fudge Frosting, page 66

Lemon Jelly Roll Cake, shown with strawberry jam filling

Plantation Marble Cake

Marble Cake became popular in the late 1800s, and was one of the first bicolor cakes. The Harlequin or Checkerboard cake was a fancy variation. Some contemporary recipes substitute chocolate for the molasses. This recipe could be found on cans of Calumet Baking Powder in 1938.

❧ Preheat oven to 350 degrees. Grease and flour one 9" x 9" x 2" cake pan. Line bottom with parchment paper.

1. In a mixing bowl, cream together butter and sugar, add eggs.
2. In another mixing bowl, mix and sift together flour, baking powder, and salt, then add to the creamed mixture alternately with milk. Divide batter into two bowls.
3. Dissolve baking soda in the molasses in a cup. Add the molasses mixture, cloves, cinnamon, and nutmeg to one bowl of batter.
4. Pour the light cake batter in bottom of cake pan. Place the dark half of the batter on top of the light batter. Swirl the dark batter gently into the light batter with a toothpick; do not over mix.
5. Bake for 35 minutes, or until top is firm to touch.

Ingredients

- 1/2 CUP BUTTER
- 1 CUP GRANULATED SUGAR
- 2 EGGS, BEATEN
- 2 CUPS ALL-PURPOSE FLOUR, SIFTED
- 2 TEASPOONS BAKING POWDER
- 1/4 TEASPOON SALT
- 1/2 CUP MILK
- 1/4 TEASPOON BAKING SODA
- 3 TABLESPOONS MOLASSES
- 1/2 TEASPOON CLOVES
- 1 TEASPOON CINNAMON
- 1/2 TEASPOON NUTMEG

Angel Food Cake

Angel Food Cake (also known as "Angel Cake") is a pristine white and fluffy cake that has been around since at least the mid to late 1800s. There is some documentation that points to Pennsylvania Dutch heritage. Save your left-over egg yolks and make a batch of pasta.

❧ Preheat oven to 350 degrees. Grease and flour one 10" tube pan.

1. In a metal mixing bowl, beat egg whites with vanilla extract and ice water until frothy, add cream of tartar and continue beating until stiff.
2. In a mixing bowl, mix and sift together sugar, flour, baking powder and salt.
3. Fold egg whites into dry ingredients.
4. Gently spoon batter into cake pan and bake for 35 minutes, or until top is golden brown and springy to touch.

Ingredients

- 11 EGG WHITES
- 1 TEASPOON VANILLA EXTRACT
- 1 TABLESPOON ICE WATER
- 1 TEASPOON CREAM OF TARTAR
- 1 1/2 CUPS GRANULATED SUGAR
- 1 CUP CAKE FLOUR, SIFTED
- 1 1/2 TEASPOONS BAKING POWDER
- 1/4 TEASPOON SALT

*Plantation Marble
Cake*

Angel Food Cake

Short Cake

Vintage Short Cake was nothing like the modern-day commercial sponge cakes that are used to hold strawberries and whipped cream. Short Cake from the mid-1800s was more biscuit-like in consistency with a very tender crumb. Top with any type of fruit sauce or Fresh Whipped Cream, page 70.

❧ Preheat oven to 375 degrees. Grease the bottoms of two 8" pie pans.

1. In a mixing bowl, cream together sugar and lard.
2. In another mixing bowl, mix and sift together the flour, baking powder and salt, then add to the creamed mixture, alternating with the milk.
3. Mix well to form a soft dough. Knead dough, divide in half and press it into the bottom of pie tins.
4. Bake 20 minutes or until golden brown.
5. Break up short cake while hot, and layer with fresh berries and whipped cream, or as shown with fruit sauce.

For the Blueberry Sauce:

In a saucepan on stove, heat until bubbling sugar, blueberries and lemon juice. Stir frequently. Simmer until thickened.

Ingredients

- 1 TABLESPOON GRANULATED SUGAR
- 4 TABLESPOONS LARD
- 2 CUPS ALL-PURPOSE FLOUR, SIFTED
- 2 TEASPOONS BAKING POWDER, HEAPING
- 1 TEASPOON SALT
- 1 CUP MILK

BLUEBERRY SAUCE:

- 1/4 CUP GRANULATED SUGAR
- 2 CUPS BLUEBERRIES
- 1 TEASPOON LEMON JUICE

Golden Sponge Cake

Known as one of the first non-yeasted cakes, Sponge Cake is a popular Passover treat. There are several derivatives from this recipe, including Chiffon Cake. Sponge Cake is a wonderful ingredient in trifles and rolled cakes because of its sturdy but airy texture.

❧ Preheat oven to 350 degrees. Grease and flour one 8" x 2" round cake pan. Line bottom with parchment paper.

1. In a metal mixing bowl, beat egg whites until stiff, then beat in the egg yolks, sugar, butter, and vanilla extract.
2. In a mixing bowl, mix and sift together flour, salt and baking powder, then add to liquid ingredients.
3. Pour batter into cake pan and bake for 25 to 30 minutes, or until top is springy and golden brown.

Ingredients

- 5 EGGS, SEPARATED
- 1 CUP GRANULATED SUGAR
- 1 TABLESPOON BUTTER, MELTED
- 1 TABLESPOON VANILLA EXTRACT
- 1 CUP ALL-PURPOSE FLOUR
- 1/4 TEASPOON SALT
- 2 TEASPOONS BAKING POWDER

Short Cake shown with Blueberry Sauce

Golden Sponge Cake, shown dusted with cinnamon and sugar

Spice Cake

There are several variations of Spice Cake that have evolved over the centuries. The addition of maple syrup made this cake popular in New Hampshire in the early 1800s. This high-rising soft cake has a crusty but sweet top.

❧ Preheat oven to 350 degrees. Grease and flour one 9" x 9" x 2" cake pan. Line bottom with parchment paper.

1. In a mixing bowl cream together butter, sugar, molasses and maple syrup. Beat in eggs and lemon extract.
2. In a separate mixing bowl, mix and sift together flour, baking powder, cinnamon, and cloves, then add alternately with milk to creamed mixture.
3. Pour batter into cake pan and bake for one hour or until top is firm to touch.

Ingredients

- 1 CUP BUTTER
- 1 1/2 CUPS GRANULATED SUGAR
- 2 TABLESPOONS MOLASSES
- 2 TABLESPOONS MAPLE SYRUP, GRADE-A DARK AMBER (US)
- 5 EGGS
- 1/2 TEASPOON LEMON EXTRACT
- 3 1/2 CUPS ALL-PURPOSE FLOUR
- 2 TEASPOONS BAKING POWDER
- 1 TEASPOON CINNAMON
- 1/2 TEASPOON CLOVES
- 1/2 CUP MILK

Lemon Pudding Cake

This cake has a soft, custard-like texture and may be served warm or chilled. Its popularity grew in the mid-1800s up until the 1930s when commercial pudding mixes became commonplace.

❧ Preheat oven to 350 degrees. Grease and flour one 8" x 2" round cake pan. Line bottom with parchment paper.

1. In a mixing bowl, cream butter and sugar and blend in the lemon zest.
2. Add egg yolks and salt and beat well.
3. Stir in flour alternately with lemon juice and milk.
4. In a metal mixing bowl, beat egg whites until stiff. Fold into batter.
5. Pour batter into cake pan and bake one hour or until the top is golden brown. Serve warm or chilled.

Ingredients

- 1 1/2 TABLESPOONS BUTTER
- 3/4 CUP GRANULATED SUGAR
- 2 TEASPOONS GRATED LEMON ZEST
- 3 EGGS, SEPARATED
- 1/4 TEASPOON SALT
- 3 TABLESPOONS ALL-PURPOSE FLOUR, SIFTED
- 1/4 CUP LEMON JUICE
- 1 CUP MILK

Spice Cake

*Lemon Pudding
Cake*

Coconut Upside Down Cake

This cake is a variation of the Pineapple Upside Down Cake, but it is not a skillet cake, although this sticky topped fluffy cake shares some similarities.

❧ Preheat oven to 325 degrees. Grease and flour one 8" x 2" round cake pan. Line bottom with parchment paper.

1. In a mixing bowl, cream together butter and 1/2 cup brown sugar until mixed, then add coconut and stir until incorporated. Press this mixture into the bottom of cake pan.
2. In another bowl, mix together 1 cup brown sugar and egg. Beat in the baking soda and sour cream. Beat in the salt and vanilla extract.
3. In a separate mixing bowl, mix and sift together flour and baking powder, then incorporate into the liquid ingredients.
4. Pour batter into the coconut-lined pan, and spread to the edges.
5. Bake for 40 minutes or until a toothpick inserted comes out clean. Cool in pan completely.
6. Invert onto serving tray. Peel away parchment paper.

Ingredients

FOR THE TOPPING:

- ◆ 2 TABLESPOONS UNSALTED BUTTER, SOFTENED
- ◆ 1/2 CUP LIGHT BROWN SUGAR
- ◆ 1 CUP COCONUT, SHREDDED, SWEETENED

FOR THE CAKE:

- ◆ 1 CUP LIGHT BROWN SUGAR
- ◆ 1 EGG
- ◆ 1 TEASPOON BAKING SODA
- ◆ 1 CUP SOUR CREAM
- ◆ 1/4 TEASPOON SALT
- ◆ 1 TEASPOON VANILLA EXTRACT
- ◆ 1 1/2 CUPS CAKE FLOUR
- ◆ 1 TEASPOON BAKING POWDER

Molasses Cake

Although Molasses Cake was eaten by the first American settlers, this recipe is from 1930. Use blackstrap molasses in this recipe as it will yield the darkest, richest cake. From a process that originated around the 1920s, blackstrap molasses is a dark, viscous material that remains after the third boiling of sugar syrup from raw sugar cane.

❧ Preheat oven to 350 degrees. Grease and flour one 9" x 9" x 2" cake pan. Line bottom with parchment paper.

1. In a mixing bowl, cream together butter and sugar.
2. Gradually beat in eggs, milk, mace and molasses.
3. In a separate mixing bowl, mix and sift together flour, baking soda, cinnamon, allspice, and cloves, then stir into liquid ingredients.
4. Pour batter into greased cake pan and bake for 50 minutes or until top is firm to touch.

Ingredients

- ◆ 2/3 CUP BUTTER
- ◆ 3/4 CUP GRANULATED SUGAR
- ◆ 2 EGGS
- ◆ 2/3 CUP MILK
- ◆ 1/4 TEASPOON MACE
- ◆ 2/3 CUP MOLASSES
- ◆ 2 1/8 CUPS ALL-PURPOSE FLOUR
- ◆ 3/4 TEASPOON BAKING SODA
- ◆ 1 TEASPOON CINNAMON
- ◆ 1/2 TEASPOON ALLSPICE
- ◆ 1/4 TEASPOON CLOVES

*Coconut Upside
Down Cake*

Molasses Cake

Dundee Cake

Many Scottish families have some version of this cake lurking in their archives. This cake dates back to the mid 1500s, and has many variations of fruit and nuts. You may find some recipes that refer to using sultanas, which are yellow raisins.

❧ Preheat oven to 325 degrees. Grease and flour one 8" x 2" round cake pan. Line bottom with parchment paper.

1. In a mixing bowl, cream together butter and sugar, then beat in eggs. Stir in chopped almonds.
2. In a separate mixing bowl, mix and sift together flour, salt, and baking powder, and then mix with raisins and currants, and add to creamed mixture.
3. Mix the orange juice with the candied orange and lemon peel in a bowl, then add to batter.
4. Mix thoroughly, and pour into cake pan. Cover top with almonds, forming a concentric circle design. Bake for 60 minutes.
5. Cover with foil as soon as cake begins to brown, at the 30-minute mark.
6. Remove from oven and brush top with warm honey.

Ingredients

- 7/8 CUP BUTTER
- 2/3 CUP GRANULATED SUGAR
- 4 EGGS
- 1/3 CUP ALMONDS, TOASTED AND CHOPPED
- 2 1/2 CUPS ALL-PURPOSE FLOUR
- 1/2 TEASPOON SALT
- 1 TEASPOON BAKING POWDER
- 1 CUP RAISINS
- 1 1/3 CUPS CURRANTS
- 2 TABLESPOONS ORANGE JUICE
- 1/3 CUP CANDIED ORANGE AND LEMON PEEL, CUT FINE
- 1/2 CUP WHOLE ALMONDS, TOASTED AND SHELLED
- 2 TABLESPOONS HONEY, WARM

Cornstarch Cake

The use of cornstarch creates a light, moist cake that rises high. Contemporary Angel Food Cake is thought to be a variant of this late 1800s recipe.

❧ Preheat oven to 350 degrees. Grease and flour two 8" x 2" round cake pans. Line bottoms with parchment paper.

1. In a metal mixing bowl, beat egg whites until stiff. Beat in half of the sugar and set aside.
2. In a mixing bowl, cream together butter, add the other half of the sugar gradually, while beating constantly.
3. In a separate mixing bowl, mix and sift together flour, cornstarch, baking powder and salt, then add alternately to creamed mixture with milk.
4. Fold in egg whites.
5. Add flavoring extract.
6. Pour into cake pans and bake for 45 minutes.

Ingredients

- 5 EGG WHITES
- 2 CUPS GRANULATED SUGAR
- 1 CUP BUTTER
- 2 CUPS ALL-PURPOSE FLOUR
- 1 CUP CORNSTARCH
- 4 1/2 TEASPOONS BAKING POWDER
- 1/4 TEASPOON SALT
- 1 CUP MILK
- 3/4 TEASPOON VANILLA OR ALMOND EXTRACT

Dundee Cake

Cornstarch Cake, shown with Cooked Vanilla Icing, page 68

Marshmallow Cake

The name of this cake is indicative of its rise rather than its flavor. There are a few variations, such as using almond extract rather than vanilla. The batter is very thick, and it may be tempting to add more milk, but resist the urge.

❧ Preheat oven to 350 degrees. Grease and flour two 8" x 2" round cake pans. Line bottoms with parchment paper.

1. In a mixing bowl, cream together shortening and sugar.
2. In a separate mixing bowl, mix and sift together flour, baking powder and salt, then add alternately with the milk to the creamed mixture.
3. In a metal mixing bowl, beat egg whites, vanilla extract and cream of tartar until stiff, then whip into batter.
4. Pour batter into cake pans and bake for 40 minutes.

Ingredients

- 1/2 CUP SHORTENING
- 1 1/2 CUPS GRANULATED SUGAR
- 2 1/2 CUPS ALL-PURPOSE FLOUR
- 3 TEASPOONS BAKING POWDER
- 1/8 TEASPOON SALT
- 3/4 CUP MILK
- 4 EGG WHITES
- 1 TEASPOON VANILLA EXTRACT
- 1/2 TEASPOON CREAM OF TARTAR

Grant Spice Cake

Grant Spice Cake is a simpler quick-bread version of the Election Cake which used yeast. Both are an American adaptation of fruit cakes.

❧ Preheat oven to 350 degrees. Grease and flour one 9" x 9" x 2" cake pan. Line bottom with parchment paper.

1. In a mixing bowl, cream together butter and sugar and gradually add egg.
2. In a separate mixing bowl, mix and sift together flour, baking soda, allspice, cloves, cinnamon and salt and add to creamed mixture, alternately with milk.
3. Stir in raisins and mix well.
4. Pour batter into cake pan and bake for 25 minutes.

Ingredients

- 1/2 CUP BUTTER
- 1 CUP GRANULATED SUGAR
- 1 EGG, WELL BEATEN
- 2 1/2 CUPS ALL-PURPOSE FLOUR
- 1 1/2 TEASPOONS BAKING SODA
- 3/4 TEASPOON ALLSPICE
- 3/4 TEASPOON CLOVES
- 1 1/2 TEASPOONS CINNAMON
- 1/2 TEASPOON SALT
- 1 CUP MILK
- 1 1/4 CUPS RAISINS, CHOPPED

Marshmallow Cake, shown with Marshmallow Frosting, page 68

Grant Spice Cake

Lightning Cake

With a light and fluffy crumb, this high-rise cake was popular in the 1930s. Double the recipe and use two 8" round cake pans for an impressive stacked cake.

❧ Preheat oven to 350 degrees. Grease and flour one 8" x 2" round cake pan. Line bottom with parchment paper.

1. In a mixing bowl, beat together egg and sugar until creamy.
2. In a separate mixing bowl, mix and sift together flour, baking powder and salt and add to eggs and sugar mixture.
3. Add milk, melted butter, lemon extract and vanilla extract, and mix well.
4. Pour into cake pan and bake for 25 minutes or until top is firm to touch.

Ingredients

- 1 EGG
- 1/2 CUP GRANULATED SUGAR
- 1 CUP ALL-PURPOSE FLOUR
- 1 TEASPOON BAKING POWDER
- 1/4 TEASPOON SALT
- 1 CUP MILK
- 3 TABLESPOONS BUTTER, MELTED
- 1/4 TEASPOON LEMON EXTRACT
- 1/2 TEASPOON VANILLA EXTRACT

Coffee Cake

Coffee cake evolved from many forms of heavy yeast bread to light and fluffy cinnamon tea cakes. Scandinavian immigrants in the early 1800s can take much of the credit for bringing this delicious pastry to America. This cake has a bread-like texture with dense but soft crumb and crunchy, rustic crust.

❧ Preheat oven to 350 degrees. Grease and flour one 10" tube pan.

1. In a mixing bowl, mix and sift together flour, sugar, baking powder, cinnamon, allspice, nutmeg and salt. Add raisins and coat with dry mixture.
2. In another mixing bowl, mix shortening together with egg and milk. Mix well and add to the dry ingredients; add more milk if necessary, to form a soft, but not sticky dough.
3. Roll out dough about 1/2" thick, divide into two long strips and twist together. Form a ring with twisted dough and lay into cake pan and sprinkle with brown sugar and nuts. Rest dough for 20 minutes.
4. Bake for 40 to 50 minutes or until toothpick inserted comes out clean.

Ingredients

- 3 CUPS ALL-PURPOSE FLOUR
- 1/2 CUP GRANULATED SUGAR
- 4 TEASPOONS BAKING POWDER
- 1/2 TEASPOON CINNAMON
- 1/2 TEASPOON ALLSPICE
- 1/4 TEASPOON NUTMEG
- 1 TEASPOON SALT
- 1 CUP RAISINS
- 3 TABLESPOONS SHORTENING, MELTED
- 1 EGG, BEATEN
- 3/4 CUP MILK
- 1/4 CUP LIGHT BROWN SUGAR
- 1/2 CUP CHOPPED NUTS

*Lightning Cake,
shown with
Marshmallow
Frosting, page 68*

Coffee Cake

Vienna Cake

Immigrants to America from Germany and Austria introduced some wonderful culinary delights. These immigrants brought with them this recipe during the mid-1800s.

Preheat oven to 325 degrees. Grease and flour one 10" tube pan.

For the Cake:

1. In a metal mixing bowl, beat egg whites until stiff and beat in 5 tablespoons of the sugar, cold water and lemon extract. Set aside.
2. In a mixing bowl, mix and sift together flour, cornstarch, baking powder and salt.
3. In a separate mixing bowl, beat together egg yolks and remaining sugar, and then add ground almonds and melted butter. Fold in egg white mixture.
4. Cut and fold in the dry ingredients.
5. Pour batter into cake pan and bake for 30 minutes.

For the Mocha Filling:

1. In a saucepan on stove, dissolve cornstarch in milk, add cocoa powder and then bring to a boil then lower heat and cook slowly for five minutes, whisking constantly.
2. Add sugar, vanilla extract and coffee. Beat well.
3. Cool completely.

To Assemble the Cake:

1. Remove cake from pan and cool completely.
2. Using a serrated bread knife, cut cake crosswise into three layers of equal thickness.
3. Spread Mocha Filling between layers and frost sides and top with remaining filling.
4. Coat entire cake with toasted almonds.

Ingredients

CAKE:

- 6 EGG WHITES
- 5 TABLESPOONS GRANULATED SUGAR
- 3 TABLESPOONS COLD WATER
- 1 TEASPOON LEMON EXTRACT
- 7/8 CUP ALL-PURPOSE FLOUR
- 1 1/2 TABLESPOONS CORNSTARCH
- 1 1/4 TEASPOONS BAKING POWDER
- 1/4 TEASPOON SALT
- 4 EGG YOLKS
- 2/3 CUP GRANULATED SUGAR
- 2 TABLESPOONS ALMONDS, TOASTED AND GROUND
- 1/4 CUP BUTTER, MELTED

MOCHA FILLING:

- 1/4 CUP CORNSTARCH
- 2 CUPS MILK
- 1/2 CUP UNSWEETENED NATURAL COCOA POWDER
- 1/2 CUP GRANULATED SUGAR
- 1/2 TEASPOON OF VANILLA EXTRACT
- 1 TABLESPOON COFFEE, BREWED STRONG

COATING:

- 1 CUP ALMONDS, TOASTED AND CHOPPED FINELY

Vienna Cake shown with toasted chopped almonds

Fudge Layer Cake

Fudge Layer Cake is a variant of the Devil's Food Cake. It is a rich cake with a dense, soft crumb.

❧ Preheat oven to 350 degrees. Grease and flour two 8" x 2" round cake pans. Line bottoms with parchment paper.

1. In a mixing bowl, cream together shortening, 1 cup sugar and vanilla extract.
2. In a double boiler, melt together chocolate, 1/3 cup sugar and boiling water until smooth.
3. Remove from heat and beat into creamed mixture.
4. Beat eggs in a separate bowl and add some of the warm chocolate mixture to temper the eggs.
5. Add egg mixture into the chocolate mixture.
6. In a separate bowl, mix and sift together flour, cream of tartar, baking soda and salt, then add to the batter alternately with the milk.
7. Pour into cake pans and bake for 25 minutes.

Ingredients

- 1/2 CUP SHORTENING
- 1 1/3 CUPS GRANULATED SUGAR
- 1/2 TEASPOON VANILLA EXTRACT
- 4 OUNCES BITTERSWEET CHOCOLATE, 60% CACAO
- 3 TABLESPOONS BOILING WATER
- 3 EGGS
- 1 3/4 CUPS ALL-PURPOSE FLOUR
- 1 TEASPOON CREAM OF TARTAR
- 1/2 TEASPOON BAKING SODA
- 1/2 TEASPOON SALT
- 1/2 CUP MILK

Gingerbread

The early European recipe for gingerbread consisted of ground almonds, honey, breadcrumbs, rosewater, sugar and ginger. The English added molasses or "treacle" in place of honey, and flour in place of the breadcrumbs. Gingerbread can take the form of bread, cookies or cake. This cake has a soft sweet crumb and crunchy top.

❧ Preheat oven to 350 degrees. Grease and flour one 10" tube pan **or** 9" x 9" x 2" cake pan. Also have available one large cookie sheet.

1. Boil molasses and butter in a large saucepan or soup pot on stove, then lower heat to medium.
2. Stir in baking soda, cinnamon, ginger and nutmeg. Mixture will rise quickly. Remove from heat.
3. Mix and sift together flour and baking powder, then add to hot mixture alternately with buttermilk. Batter will be hot.
4. In a separate bowl, beat egg then add some of the hot batter to temper. Add egg to batter; mix well.
5. Pour into cake pan and place cookie sheet under baking pan as batter will continue to rise. Bake for one hour or until top is crusty and firm to touch.

Ingredients

- 2 CUPS MOLASSES
- 3/4 CUP BUTTER
- 2 TEASPOONS BAKING SODA
- 1 TEASPOON CINNAMON
- 1 TEASPOON POWDERED GINGER
- 1/2 TEASPOON NUTMEG
- 3 CUPS ALL-PURPOSE FLOUR
- 2 TEASPOONS BAKING POWDER
- 1 CUP BUTTERMILK
- 1 EGG, BEATEN

Fudge Layer Cake, shown with Chocolate Flavored American Buttercream Frosting, page 66

Gingerbread

Dark Fruit Cake

Fruit cakes became popular in the Middle Ages, when dried fruits and spices arrived in England, and were mostly used for celebrations due to the expense and time in making them. Monks have made fruit cakes for centuries to raise money for their monasteries. Mail order fruit cakes became available in America around 1913. This recipe is from 1848, and it has a Caribbean influence (where it's also called "black cake") from the use of dark rum. Use bourbon or brandy in place of the rum if you prefer. Fruit cakes may be eaten right away or stored and allowed to age.

1. Soak raisins, currants, citron, dates and cherries overnight covered in 1 1/2 cups of the dark rum in a glass or non-reactive bowl. Fruits will absorb most of the liquid.
2. The next day, using a mortar and pestle, pulverize almonds into paste with rose water and set aside.
3. In a cup, dissolve baking soda into molasses. Mix together the soaked fruits and ground almond mixture, baking soda and molasses mixture in a mixing bowl. Add orange zest.
4. In a mixing bowl, cream together butter and brown sugar. Add eggs and orange juice while mixing.

❧ Preheat oven to 325 degrees. Prepare a light colored 10" tube pan: Grease the sides and center tube of pan, then line with two layers of parchment paper strips. Do not use foil.

5. In a separate mixing bowl, mix and sift together flour, baking powder, allspice, cinnamon, cloves, nutmeg, mace and ginger. Combine fruit with nut mixture in small amounts.
6. Pour batter into tube pan. Top with pecan halves.
7. Bake for one hour. When toothpick comes out clean, remove from oven, spritz top of cake with 1/4 cup rum and allow to cool in pan for one hour. When cake is completely cooled, seal in an air-tight food-safe container in a cool, dark place. Every two days, feel the cake and if it is dry, spritz with 1/4 cup rum. The flavor will enhance considerably over the next week.

Ingredients

- 3 CUPS DARK RUM
- 1/2 CUP RAISINS
- 1/2 CUP CURRANTS
- 1/2 CUP CITRON
- 1/2 CUP DATES, CHOPPED
- 1/2 CUP CHERRIES, DRIED, CHOPPED
- 1/8 CUP SHELLED ALMONDS, BLANCHED
- 1/8 CUP ROSE WATER
- 1 TEASPOON BAKING SODA
- 1/4 CUP MOLASSES
- 1 TABLESPOON ORANGE ZEST
- 1 CUP BUTTER
- 1 1/2 CUPS DARK BROWN SUGAR
- 6 EGGS, BEATEN
- 1/4 CUP ORANGE JUICE
- 1 CUP ALL-PURPOSE FLOUR
- 1 TEASPOON BAKING POWDER
- 1/4 TEASPOON ALLSPICE
- 1/4 TEASPOON CINNAMON
- 1/4 TEASPOON CLOVES
- 1/4 TEASPOON NUTMEG
- 1/4 TEASPOON MACE
- 1/4 TEASPOON GINGER, POWDERED
- 1 CUP PECAN HALVES

Dark Fruit Cake

Harvard Cake

This dense, sticky sweet cake is a high-riser and is very tender and moist. Harvard Cake was popular in the early 1900s and is a variant of Spice Cake. Use fresh dates (not dried) for extra moistness.

✿ Preheat oven to 350 degrees. Grease and flour one 9" x 9" x 2" cake pan. Line bottom with parchment paper.

1. Cream together butter and brown sugar in a mixing bowl. Beat in egg yolks.
2. In a separate mixing bowl, mix and sift together flour, baking soda, cinnamon and nutmeg.
3. Add the sifted mixture to the creamed mixture alternately with the milk.
4. Coat dates with a dusting of flour and add to batter. Stir well.
5. Pour batter into cake pan. Bake for 35 to 40 minutes, or until toothpick inserted comes out clean.

Ingredients

- ◆ 1/2 CUP BUTTER
- ◆ 2 CUPS BROWN SUGAR
- ◆ 2 EGG YOLKS, BEATEN
- ◆ 2 CUPS ALL-PURPOSE FLOUR
- ◆ 1 TEASPOON BAKING SODA
- ◆ 1/2 TEASPOON CINNAMON
- ◆ 1/2 TEASPOON NUTMEG
- ◆ 1 CUP SOUR MILK
- ◆ 1/2 POUND DATES, PITTED AND CUT INTO SMALL PIECES

Gold Cake

Gold Cake was also known as King's Cake, and has a rich lemony yellow color with a soft and fluffy texture. Often found with Silver Cake or Angel Food in older cookbooks, it utilizes the left-over yolks not needed in cakes made only with egg whites.

✿ Preheat oven to 350 degrees. Grease and flour one 8" x 2" round cake pan. Line bottom with parchment paper.

1. In a mixing bowl, cream together butter and sugar.
2. Add egg yolks and orange extract and beat well.
3. In a separate mixing bowl, mix and sift together flour and baking powder and add alternately with milk to creamed ingredients.
4. Pour batter into cake pan and bake for 35 to 40 minutes, or until toothpick inserted comes out clean.

Ingredients

- ◆ 1/4 CUP BUTTER
- ◆ 1/2 CUP GRANULATED SUGAR
- ◆ 5 EGG YOLKS
- ◆ 1 TEASPOON ORANGE EXTRACT
- ◆ 7/8 CUP ALL-PURPOSE FLOUR
- ◆ 1 1/2 TEASPOONS BAKING POWDER
- ◆ 1/2 CUP MILK

Harvard Cake

*Gold Cake, shown
with Vanilla Glaze,
page 66*

Ribbon Cake

This impressive stacked cake made its appearance around the 1920s and many variants followed. Use any flavor of fruit jam or custard between layers.

❧ Preheat oven to 350 degrees. Grease and flour four 8" x 2" round cake pans. Line bottoms with parchment paper.

1. In a mixing bowl, cream together butter and sugar. Add eggs and beat well.
2. In a separate mixing bowl, mix and sift together flour, baking soda and salt. Add to the creamed mixture alternately with the milk.
3. Divide batter into two bowls.
4. In one half, mix in molasses, raisins, cinnamon, allspice, cloves, nutmeg and citron.
5. Pour dark batter into two cake pans. Then pour light batter into two additional pans. Two pans should have the light batter and two should have the dark batter.
6. Bake for 20 minutes, or until top is firm to touch.
7. Assemble the four layers together while warm, alternating light and dark layers, spreading fruit jam between layers. If you use custard, allow cake to cool completely before applying.

Ingredients

- ◆ 2/3 CUP BUTTER
- ◆ 2 CUPS GRANULATED SUGAR
- ◆ 3 EGGS
- ◆ 3 CUPS ALL-PURPOSE FLOUR
- ◆ 1 TEASPOON BAKING SODA
- ◆ 1/4 TEASPOON SALT
- ◆ 1 CUP MILK
- ◆ 1 TABLESPOON MOLASSES
- ◆ 1 CUP RAISINS, CHOPPED
- ◆ 1 TEASPOON CINNAMON
- ◆ 1/2 TEASPOON ALLSPICE
- ◆ 1/2 TEASPOON CLOVES
- ◆ 1/4 TEASPOON NUTMEG
- ◆ 1/4 CUP DICED CITRON
- ◆ 2 CUPS FRUIT JAM OR CUSTARD

White Velvet Cake

This cake is from the late 1800s. The recipe is in stark contrast to Red Velvet Cake of the 1930s as it does not contain chocolate, coffee or any coloring. You might find many cakes from this era named Velvet. The term "velvet" denoted any cake with an especially soft crumb.

❧ Preheat oven to 350 degrees. Grease and flour one 8" x 2" round cake pan. Line bottom with parchment paper.

1. In a mixing bowl, cream butter and add sugar and egg yolks gradually until well beaten. Add water.
2. In a separate mixing bowl, mix and sift together flour, cornstarch, baking powder and salt, then add to creamed mixture.
3. In a metal mixing bowl, beat egg whites until stiff and fold into batter.
4. Pour batter into cake pan and bake for 40 minutes.
5. Remove from oven and cover with almonds and powdered sugar.

Ingredients

- ◆ 1/2 CUP BUTTER
- ◆ 1 1/2 CUPS GRANULATED SUGAR
- ◆ 4 EGG YOLKS
- ◆ 1/2 CUP COLD WATER
- ◆ 1 1/2 CUPS ALL-PURPOSE FLOUR
- ◆ 1/2 CUP CORNSTARCH
- ◆ 4 TEASPOONS BAKING POWDER
- ◆ 1/2 TEASPOON SALT
- ◆ 4 EGG WHITES
- ◆ 1/3 CUP ALMONDS, CHOPPED
- ◆ 1 TABLESPOON POWDERED SUGAR

Ribbon Cake,
shown with
Strawberry Jam

White Velvet Cake
shown topped with
sliced almonds and
powdered sugar

Date Cake

Dates have been used in cakes for thousands of years. They add a certain moistness and sweet flavor to cakes and are very healthy. Use fresh dates (not dried) in this recipe for a moist and tender bite.

❧ Preheat oven to 350 degrees. Grease and flour one 9" x 5" x 2-3/4" loaf pan. Line bottom with parchment paper.

1. Soak dates in hot water and baking soda in a bowl. Allow to cool.
2. In a mixing bowl, cream together shortening and sugar, and then add egg. Beat until creamy.
3. In a separate mixing bowl, mix and sift together flour, cinnamon and salt and add to creamed mixture.
4. Stir in the dates, baking soda and water mixture and pecans; incorporate well.
5. Pour batter into loaf pan and bake for one hour.

Ingredients

- 1 CUP DATES, CHOPPED
- 1 CUP HOT WATER
- 1 TEASPOON BAKING SODA
- 1/4 CUP SHORTENING
- 1 CUP GRANULATED SUGAR
- 1 EGG
- 1 1/2 CUPS ALL-PURPOSE FLOUR
- 1 TEASPOON CINNAMON
- 1/2 TEASPOON SALT
- 1/2 CUP PECANS, CHOPPED

Queen's Cake

Queen's Cake was popular in the mid-1800s in Great Britain, during Queen Victoria's reign. It is dense with a soft muffin-like crumb.

❧ Preheat oven to 350 degrees. Grease and flour one 8" x 2" round cake pan. Line bottom with parchment paper.

1. In a mixing bowl, cream butter until soft and light.
2. In another mixing bowl, mix and sift together flour, salt and baking soda and add to butter. Add lemon juice.
3. Separately, in a metal mixing bowl, beat egg whites until stiff; beat in sugar. Fold into batter.
4. Pour batter into cake pan and bake for 50 minutes or until top is firm to touch.

Ingredients

- 2/3 CUP BUTTER
- 1 2/3 CUPS ALL-PURPOSE FLOUR
- 1/4 TEASPOON SALT
- 1/4 TEASPOON BAKING SODA
- 1 1/2 TEASPOONS LEMON JUICE
- 6 EGG WHITES
- 1 1/4 CUPS POWDERED SUGAR

Date Cake

*Queen's Cake,
shown with
Vanilla Glaze,
page 66*

Banana Cake

Bananas were somewhat new to American homes in the 1880s, and banana breads and cakes became a regular household staple by the 1930s. Banana Cake was touted as quick bread that didn't require yeast by the baking powder companies. This recipe is similar to contemporary banana bread with a soft, dense crumb and sweet crust.

Preheat oven to 350 degrees. Grease and flour one 10" tube pan.

1. In a mixing bowl, cream together shortening and granulated sugar.
2. Add salt and vanilla extract.
3. Add eggs, beating well after each, until light and fluffy.
4. Add milk and bananas.
5. In a separate mixing bowl, mix and sift together cake four, baking powder and baking soda and slowly add to wet ingredients.
6. Pour batter into cake pan. Bake for 40 minutes or until top is firm to touch.
7. Dust with powdered sugar when cool.

Ingredients

- 1/2 CUP SHORTENING
- 1 1/2 CUPS GRANULATED SUGAR
- 1/2 TEASPOON SALT
- 1 TEASPOON VANILLA EXTRACT
- 2 EGGS
- 1/4 CUP SOUR MILK OR BUTTERMILK
- 1 CUP MASHED BANANAS
- 2 CUPS CAKE FLOUR
- 1/2 TEASPOON BAKING POWDER
- 3/4 TEASPOON BAKING SODA
- 1 TABLESPOON POWDERED SUGAR

Pudding Cake

This cake originated in England and arrived in America during the 1700s. It has a dense crumb and crusty sweet top, and is delicious on its own or with the homemade Bourbon Pudding.

Preheat oven to 350 degrees. Grease and flour one 8" x 2" round cake pan. Line bottom with parchment paper.

1. In a mixing bowl, cream together butter and sugar, add eggs and vanilla extract.
2. In a separate mixing bowl, mix and sift together flour and baking powder and add to the creamed mixture alternately with the milk.
3. Pour batter into cake pan and bake for 40 minutes, or until top is firm to touch.

For the Pudding:

1. Place milk in a double boiler, then add cornstarch over moderate heat. Add sugar.
2. Stir and cook until thickened. Remove from heat.
3. Add bourbon and serve pudding with cake.

Ingredients

- 1/2 CUP BUTTER
- 1 1/4 CUPS GRANULATED SUGAR
- 3 EGGS
- 1/2 TEASPOON VANILLA EXTRACT
- 3 CUPS ALL-PURPOSE FLOUR
- 1 1/2 TEASPOONS BAKING POWDER
- 1/2 CUP MILK

PUDDING:

- 2 CUPS MILK
- 1/2 CUP CORNSTARCH
- 1/2 CUP GRANULATED SUGAR
- 1/2 CUP BOURBON

Banana Cake shown dusted with powdered sugar

Pudding Cake

Cinnamon Supper Cake

This recipe is from the early 1800s and is a quick and easy cake to bake. It has a fluffy crumb, and the topping gives this soft cake a sweet finish.

🍀 Preheat oven to 375 degrees. Grease and flour one 8" x 2" round cake pan. Line bottom with parchment paper.

1. In a mixing bowl, cream together shortening and granulated sugar until fluffy. Add egg, beat well. Add vanilla extract and milk.
2. In a separate mixing bowl, mix and sift together flour, baking powder, and salt, then add to batter. Beat until smooth.
3. Pour batter into cake pan and bake for 20 to 25 minutes.
4. Remove from oven. Immediately spread top with butter, then mix and sift powdered sugar and cinnamon over cake. Serve warm.

Ingredients

- 1/4 CUP SHORTENING
- 3/4 CUP GRANULATED SUGAR
- 1 EGG
- 1 TEASPOON VANILLA EXTRACT
- 1/2 CUP MILK
- 1 CUP ALL-PURPOSE FLOUR, SIFTED
- 1 1/2 TEASPOONS BAKING POWDER
- 1/4 TEASPOON SALT
- 1 TABLESPOON BUTTER, SOFTENED
- 3 TABLESPOONS POWDERED SUGAR
- 1 TEASPOON CINNAMON

Pound Cake

This cake originates sometime in the late 1700s and is named for the equal weight of its ingredients. This dense, moist cake tastes wonderful on its own, dipped in Chocolate Ganache, page 70, or served with fruit compote.

🍀 Preheat oven to 300 degrees. Grease and flour two 9" x 5" x 2-3/4" loaf pans. Line bottoms with parchment paper.

1. In a mixing bowl, cream together butter and sugar, add egg yolks and brandy and beat well, until lemon-colored.
2. In a separate mixing bowl, mix and sift together flour and mace and add to creamed mixture and beat vigorously for at least seven minutes.
3. In a metal mixing bowl, beat egg whites until stiff and fold into batter.
4. Pour batter into loaf pans and bake for 90 minutes, or until toothpick inserted comes out clean.

Ingredients

- 2 CUPS BUTTER
- 2 CUPS GRANULATED SUGAR
- 10 EGGS, SEPARATED
- 2 TABLESPOONS BRANDY
- 2 CUPS ALL-PURPOSE FLOUR
- 1/2 TEASPOON MACE

Cinnamon Supper Cake shown with melted butter, powdered sugar and cinnamon

Pound Cake

Chocolate Icebox Cake

Ice box cakes, charlottes and trifles all share a common history, and were introduced during World War I. They were popular with housewives because one could use store-bought cookies, whipped cream and custards to assemble an impressive, tasty cake. They were usually pieced together in molds and chilled overnight. My mother also had a banana version of this recipe, in which she used vanilla cookies and homemade banana cream pudding.

For the Wafers:

1. In a mixing bowl, cream together butter and sugar.
2. In a separate mixing bowl, mix and sift together flour, cocoa, salt, and baking soda, then add to creamed mixture.
3. Combine the milk and vanilla extract in a another bowl, then add the milk and vanilla extract to dough and mix until blended (a pastry blender will come in handy here).
4. Knead and roll dough into a firm ball. Wrap dough in plastic and refrigerate for at least an hour.

   ❧ Preheat oven to 350 degrees. Line several cookie sheets with parchment paper.

5. Quarter the dough and roll out each quarter on a floured surface. Roll evenly 1/4" thick.
6. Cut out cookies with a round biscuit or cookie cutter 2" in diameter. You should have a total of 70 cookies.
7. Place slices on cookie sheets about two inches apart to allow for spreading. Bake 12 to 15 minutes or until crisp. Cool completely.

For the Chocolate Filling:

In a saucepan on stove, dissolve the cornstarch in milk, add the cocoa powder and then bring to a boil and reduce heat, then cook slowly for five minutes, whisking constantly. Add sugar and vanilla extract. Beat well. Cool completely.

To Assemble the Cake:

Spread a small amount of filling on a cake plate or inside a trifle bowl. Place a layer of six wafers in a circle and 1 in the center; use 7 cookies for each layer. Spread a layer of filling over layer of cookies and repeat. Stack and alternate between wafers and filling as you build. Refrigerate overnight before serving.

Ingredients

CHOCOLATE WAFERS:

- 14 TABLESPOONS BUTTER, SOFTENED
- 1 CUP GRANULATED SUGAR
- 1 1/2 CUPS ALL-PURPOSE FLOUR
- 3/4 CUP UNSWEETENED NATURAL COCOA POWDER
- 1/4 TEASPOON SALT
- 1/4 TEASPOON BAKING SODA
- 3 TABLESPOONS MILK
- 1 TEASPOON VANILLA EXTRACT

CHOCOLATE FILLING:

- 1/4 CUP CORNSTARCH
- 2 CUPS MILK
- 1/2 CUP UNSWEETENED NATURAL COCOA POWDER
- 1/2 CUP GRANULATED SUGAR
- 1/2 TEASPOON OF VANILLA EXTRACT

Chocolate Icebox Cake, shown using 1½ recipes' worth of cookies and filling (approximately 105 cookies)

Snow Cake

This fluffy, white cake has a soft crumb with a hint of vanilla. Snow Cake is an old-fashioned wedding cake from the early 1900s. Double this recipe for an impressive two-layer creation.

❧ Preheat oven to 350 degrees. Grease and flour one 8" x 2" round cake pan. Line bottom with parchment paper.

1. In a metal mixing bowl, beat together 1/2 cup sugar and egg whites until stiff and set aside.
2. In a separate mixing bowl, cream butter and 1/2 cup sugar.
3. Separately in another bowl, mix and sift together flour, baking powder and salt, then add to creamed mixture alternately with milk.
4. Fold in egg whites. Add flavoring extract.
5. Pour batter into cake pan and bake for 45 minutes.

Ingredients

- ◆ **2 EGG WHITES**
- ◆ **1 CUP GRANULATED SUGAR**
- ◆ **1/4 CUP BUTTER**
- ◆ **1 2/3 CUPS ALL-PURPOSE FLOUR**
- ◆ **2 1/2 TEASPOONS BAKING POWDER**
- ◆ **1/4 TEASPOON SALT**
- ◆ **1/2 CUP MILK**
- ◆ **1/2 TEASPOON VANILLA OR ALMOND EXTRACT**

Husband's Cake

Also known as the "Mystery Cake" this cake was part of a marketing campaign by the soup companies of the 1920s. The tomato soup does not dominate the flavor of this cake; most people only note how soft the texture of the crumb is in addition to the lovely spicy flavor.

❧ Preheat oven to 350 degrees. Grease and flour one 10" tube pan.

1. In a mixing bowl, cream together margarine and sugar until smooth.
2. In a separate mixing bowl, mix and sift together flour, baking powder, baking soda, cinnamon, nutmeg, ground cloves and salt.
3. In another bowl, add water to the tomato soup and mix well.
4. Add sifted dry ingredients to creamed margarine and sugar, alternately with soup mixture.
5. Quickly stir in raisins and walnuts.
6. Pour batter into cake pan and bake for one hour or until toothpick inserted comes out clean. Cool in pan 10 minutes and turn out onto wire rack.

Ingredients

- ◆ **12 TABLESPOONS MARGARINE**
- ◆ **1 1/2 CUPS GRANULATED SUGAR**
- ◆ **3 CUPS ALL-PURPOSE FLOUR, SIFTED**
- ◆ **3 TEASPOONS BAKING POWDER**
- ◆ **1 TEASPOON BAKING SODA**
- ◆ **2 TEASPOONS CINNAMON**
- ◆ **2 TEASPOONS NUTMEG**
- ◆ **1 1/4 TEASPOONS GROUND CLOVES**
- ◆ **3/4 TEASPOON SALT**
- ◆ **3/4 CUP WATER**
- ◆ **1 CUP TOMATO SOUP**
- ◆ **1 1/2 CUPS RAISINS**
- ◆ **1 1/2 CUPS WALNUTS, CHOPPED**

Snow Cake, shown with Cooked Vanilla Icing, page 68

Husband's Cake

Red Velvet Cake

This cake surfaced sometime in the 1930s. The chemical reaction between alkaline and acid ingredients is thought to have caused the red tint to this cake. Red Velvet cake was popularized by the Waldorf-Astoria Hotel. Contemporary ingredients make the bright red nearly impossible to achieve without food coloring or paste.

❧ Preheat oven to 350 degrees. Grease and flour two 8" x 2" round" cake pans. Line bottoms with parchment paper.

1. In a cup, mix coffee with cocoa and food coloring to make a paste and allow to cool.
2. In a mixing bowl, cream together sugar and shortening.
3. Beat in eggs and vanilla extract. Combine cocoa mixture with creamed mixture and beat in vinegar.
4. In a separate mixing bowl, mix and sift together flour, baking soda and salt. Add to creamed mixture alternating with milk.
5. Pour batter into cake pans and bake for 40 minutes.

Ingredients

- 4 TABLESPOONS COFFEE, BOILING HOT
- 4 TABLESPOONS UNSWEETENED NATURAL COCOA POWDER
- 1 1/2 TEASPOONS RED FOOD COLORING
- 1 1/2 CUPS GRANULATED SUGAR
- 1 1/2 CUPS SHORTENING
- 2 EGGS
- 1 TEASPOON VANILLA EXTRACT
- 1 TABLESPOON VINEGAR
- 2 CUPS CAKE FLOUR
- 1 TEASPOON BAKING SODA
- 3/4 TEASPOON SALT
- 1 CUP BUTTERMILK

Hot Milk Cake

This heritage cake gets its distinctive flavor from scalded milk, and is a high-riser with a light, fluffy crumb and sweet crust.

❧ Preheat oven to 350 degrees. Grease and flour one 8" x 2" round cake pan. Line bottom with parchment paper.

1. In a mixing bowl, beat eggs, and add sugar and lemon extract gradually.
2. Separately, mix and sift together the flour, baking powder and salt.
3. Fold into beaten eggs and sugar mixture.
4. In a saucepan on stove, heat milk and butter to scalding, just short of boiling point (180 degrees), then remove from heat and add to batter and mix quickly.
5. Pour batter into cake pan. Bake for 40 minutes.

Ingredients

- 2 EGGS
- 1 CUP GRANULATED SUGAR
- 3/4 TEASPOON LEMON EXTRACT
- 1 CUP ALL-PURPOSE FLOUR
- 1 TEASPOON BAKING POWDER
- 1/4 TEASPOON SALT
- 1/2 CUP MILK
- 1 TEASPOON BUTTER

Red Velvet Cake, shown with Cream Cheese Frosting, page 68

Hot Milk Cake, shown with Cooked Vanilla Icing, page 68

Priscilla Cake

The Modern Priscilla Cookbook was published by the Priscilla Publishing Company in Boston as an off-shoot of Modern Priscilla Magazine (1887-1930). The book boasted 1,000 recipes that were widely circulated and adapted by many housewives of the time, including my grandmother. She kept a clipping of this recipe from the magazine and had notes scrawled around it with suggestions for improvement. This is Grandma's variation.

❧ Preheat oven to 350 degrees. Grease and flour one 8" x 2" round cake pan. Line bottom with parchment paper.

1. In a mixing bowl, cream butter and 3/4 cup of the sugar.
2. In a separate mixing bowl, add remaining 3/4 cup sugar to egg and then combine with creamed mixture.
3. In a separate mixing bowl, mix and sift together flour, baking powder and salt, then add to creamed mixture alternately with milk.
4. Pour batter into cake pan and bake for 50 minutes or until top is firm to touch.

Ingredients

- 1/2 CUP BUTTER
- 1 1/2 CUPS GRANULATED SUGAR
- 5 EGGS, WELL BEATEN
- 1 TEASPOON VANILLA EXTRACT
- 2 1/3 CUPS ALL-PURPOSE FLOUR
- 2 1/4 TEASPOONS BAKING POWDER
- 1/2 TEASPOON SALT
- 1/2 CUP MILK

Sunshine Cake

Lemony, light and fluffy, this sunny cake with a soft crumb was popular in the late 1920s and may have been a variant of the angel food cake. Top with Vanilla Glaze, page 66, mixed with 3 tablespoons orange or lemon zest and you'll have an even "sunnier" cake.

❧ Preheat oven to 350 degrees. Grease and flour one 8" x 2" round cake pan. Line bottom with parchment paper.

1. In a mixing bowl, beat the egg yolks, sugar, and lemon extract.
2. In a metal mixing bowl, beat egg whites until stiff.
3. In a separate mixing bowl, mix and sift together the flour and cream of tartar, then add to the egg yolks, sugar and lemon extract mixture.
4. Fold egg whites into batter.
5. Pour batter into cake pan and bake for 50 minutes.

Ingredients

- 7 EGG YOLKS
- 1 1/2 CUPS POWDERED SUGAR
- 1 TEASPOON LEMON EXTRACT
- 10 EGG WHITES
- 1 CUP CAKE FLOUR
- 7/8 TEASPOON CREAM OF TARTAR

Priscilla Cake

*Sunshine Cake,
shown dusted
with powdered
sugar*

Orange Cake with Maple Penuche

This sponge cake recipe from my mother's notes was dated 1928. It is a light, fluffy sponge cake, which works well in contrast to the sweet maple filling and crunch of the almonds. In southern regions, pecans were used, and in New England, almonds were preferred.

❧ Preheat oven to 350 degrees. Grease one 9" x 13" x 1" jelly roll pan (a cookie sheet will work). Line bottom with parchment paper.

For the Penuche Filling:

1. In a saucepan on stove starting at medium heat, stirring constantly, slowly bring to a boil brown sugar, granulated sugar, milk, 2 tablespoons butter, maple syrup, and salt. Boil for one minute, and continue to stir.
2. Remove from heat and allow to cool. When lukewarm, stir in vanilla.
3. When cooled completely, add milk, powdered sugar and 8 tablespoons butter, then whip until creamy. Add more milk, if needed, to reach desired consistency.

For the Cake:

1. In a mixing bowl, cream together sugar and butter. Add water, egg yolks, orange juice and orange zest. Beat well.
2. In a metal mixing bowl, beat egg whites until stiff.
3. In a separate mixing bowl, mix and sift together flour, baking soda and cream of tartar, then add to creamed mixture.
4. Fold egg whites into batter.
5. Spread batter evenly in the pan, and bake for 25 minutes. Turn pan around at 13 minutes to ensure even cooking.

To Assemble the Cake:

1. As soon as cake is done, remove from oven and create the layers by slicing it into three equal-sized pieces.
2. Spread Penuche Filling over one layer, then sprinkle with almonds.
3. Place the second layer over the first and repeat. Add the third layer and top with more Penuche Filling and almonds. Serve warm.

Ingredients

PENUCHE FILLING:

♦ 1 CUP BROWN SUGAR

♦ 1/2 CUP GRANULATED SUGAR

♦ 1/3 CUP MILK

♦ 2 TABLESPOONS BUTTER

♦ 2 TABLESPOONS MAPLE SYRUP, GRADE-A DARK AMBER (US)

♦ 1/4 TEASPOON SALT

♦ 1/2 TEASPOON VANILLA

♦ 1 1/2 CUPS POWDERED SUGAR

♦ 8 TABLESPOONS BUTTER, SOFTENED

♦ 1 TABLESPOON MILK

♦ 1 CUP ALMONDS, TOASTED AND CHOPPED OR SLICED

CAKE:

♦ 2 CUPS GRANULATED SUGAR

♦ 1/2 CUP BUTTER

♦ 1/2 CUP WATER

♦ 5 EGGS, SEPARATED

♦ 1/4 CUP ORANGE JUICE

♦ 3 TABLESPOONS ORANGE ZEST

♦ 2 CUPS ALL-PURPOSE FLOUR

♦ 1/2 TEASPOON BAKING SODA

♦ 1 TEASPOON CREAM OF TARTAR

Orange Cake with Maple Penuche

Texas Sheet Cake

This sheet or "sheath" cake as it was interchangeably referred to gained popularity in the US during the early 1900s when the price of chocolate diminished. Although Texas can take claim to the cake in name and size, there is no proof that it originated in the Lone Star state. The crumb is soft and light, and the warm frosting with nuts adds a pleasing, decadent crunch.

❧ Preheat oven to 375 degrees. Grease one 15" x 11" x 1" cookie sheet. Line bottom with parchment paper.

For the Cake:

1. In a saucepan on stove over medium heat, mix together 8 tablespoons butter, shortening, water and cocoa powder and cook until bubbling; stir constantly. Remove from heat.
2. In a mixing bowl, mix and sift together flour, sugar, and salt, then beat into cocoa mixture until well integrated.
3. Add buttermilk, baking soda, vanilla extract and eggs. Mix well.
4. Pour batter onto sheet pan and spread evenly. Bake for 20-25 minutes. Turn pan around at 10 minutes to ensure even cooking.
5. Remove from oven and frost immediately while hot.

For the Frosting:

1. In a saucepan on stove over medium heat, stir together butter, milk, and cocoa powder and cook until bubbling. Remove from heat.
2. Beat in powdered sugar, vanilla extract and nuts.
3. Pour over cake immediately after cake is removed from oven.
4. Spread to edges of cake.

Ingredients

- 8 TABLESPOONS BUTTER
- 1/2 CUP SHORTENING
- 1 CUP WATER
- 4 TABLESPOONS UNSWEETENED NATURAL COCOA POWDER
- 2 CUPS ALL-PURPOSE FLOUR
- 2 CUPS GRANULATED SUGAR
- 1/2 TEASPOON SALT
- 1/2 CUP BUTTERMILK
- 1 TEASPOON BAKING SODA
- 1 1/2 TEASPOONS VANILLA EXTRACT
- 2 EGGS

FOR FROSTING:

- 8 TABLESPOONS BUTTER
- 7 TABLESPOONS MILK
- 4 TABLESPOONS UNSWEETENED NATURAL COCOA POWDER
- 2 CUPS POWDERED SUGAR
- 1 1/2 TEASPOONS VANILLA EXTRACT
- 1 CUP NUTS, CHOPPED AND TOASTED (PECANS, WALNUTS, ALMONDS OR MIXED)

Texas Sheet Cake

American Buttercream Frosting

In a mixing bowl, beat together powdered sugar, butter, 4-1/2 tablespoons of the milk, vanilla extract and salt until combined and fluffy. Add additional milk, one teaspoon at a time until desired consistency is reached.

If you desire rich chocolate buttercream, add 3 ounces of melted bittersweet chocolate (60% cacao) to this recipe. If you desire a pure white frosting, substitute half of the butter with solid vegetable shortening and use clear vanilla extract. Makes 3 cups.

Ingredients

- 6 CUPS POWDERED SUGAR, SIFTED
- 16 TABLESPOONS BUTTER, ROOM TEMPERATURE
- 4 1/2 TABLESPOONS MILK, PLUS MORE, IF NECESSARY
- 2 TEASPOONS VANILLA EXTRACT
- 1/4 TEASPOON SALT

Chocolate Fudge Frosting

Melt butter and chocolate together on top of a double boiler. Remove from heat and beat in salt, powdered sugar, evaporated milk and vanilla extract. Refrigerate for about an hour and then beat until the icing is thick and creamy. Makes enough frosting to cover a double-layer 8" round cake.

Ingredients

- 1/2 CUP BUTTER
- 4 OUNCES BITTERSWEET CHOCOLATE, 60% CACAO, CHOPPED FINE
- 1/4 TEASPOON SALT
- 2 CUPS POWDERED SUGAR, SIFTED
- 1/3 CUP EVAPORATED MILK
- 1 TEASPOON VANILLA EXTRACT

Vanilla Glaze

Sift powdered sugar into a medium size bowl. Stir in melted butter into powdered sugar. Add milk and flavoring. Beat until smooth and creamy, adding more milk in small amounts if necessary. Drizzle over warm cake. Makes about 1 to 2 cups.

Ingredients

- 2 CUPS POWDERED SUGAR
- 1/4 CUP BUTTER, MELTED
- 2 TABLESPOONS MILK, OR MORE (MAY USE HEAVY CREAM FOR RICHER GLAZE)
- 1 TEASPOON VANILLA EXTRACT (MAY SUBSTITUTE OTHER FLAVORINGS)

American Buttercream Frosting

Chocolate Fudge Frosting

Vanilla Glaze

Cooked Vanilla Icing

In a saucepan on stove, combine cream, flour and salt. Cook over medium heat for 5 minutes, stirring constantly, until mixture thickens and bubbles. Cool for at least one hour.

Separately, beat together powdered sugar, butter and vanilla extract until creamy. Gradually add cooled flour mixture, and then shortening. Beat until light and fluffy. Makes enough frosting to cover a double-layer 8" round cake.

Ingredients

- 2/3 CUP HEAVY CREAM
- 2 TABLESPOONS ALL-PURPOSE FLOUR, SIFTED
- 1/4 TEASPOON SALT
- 2/3 CUP POWDERED SUGAR, SIFTED
- 2/3 CUP BUTTER, SOFTENED
- 1 1/2 TEASPOONS VANILLA EXTRACT
- 2/3 CUP SHORTENING

Cream Cheese Frosting

In a mixing bowl, beat together powdered sugar, cream cheese, vanilla extract, butter and milk until creamy and smooth. Add more milk or powdered sugar until desired consistency and taste is reached. Makes enough frosting to cover a double-layer 8" round cake.

Ingredients

- 3 CUPS POWDERED SUGAR, SIFTED
- 4 OUNCES CREAM CHEESE, SOFTENED AT ROOM TEMPERATURE
- 1 TEASPOON VANILLA EXTRACT
- 4 TABLESPOONS BUTTER, SOFTENED
- 2 TABLESPOONS MILK

Marshmallow Frosting

In a saucepan on the stove, bring to boil water, sugar, and cream of tartar until bubbling, about 5 minutes, stirring constantly. Remove from heat. In a metal mixing bowl, beat egg whites until stiff. Add the mixture of boiled water, sugar and cream of tartar in small spoonfuls and beat for five minutes. Add flavoring and continue beating for an additional three minutes. Use within 24 hours; will "deflate" within a day, especially if fats, such as chocolate, are added. Makes enough frosting to cover a double-layer 8" round cake.

Ingredients

- 1/3 CUP OF WATER
- 1 CUP GRANULATED SUGAR
- 1/2 TEASPOON CREAM OF TARTAR
- 4 EGG WHITES
- 1 TEASPOON VANILLA EXTRACT OR OTHER FLAVORING AS DESIRED

Cooked Vanilla Icing

Cream Cheese Frosting

Marshmallow Frosting

Chocolate Ganache

Heat heavy cream until bubbling in a saucepan on stove. Add chocolate and coffee granules to the hot cream and allow to melt for one minute. Remove from heat. Stir slowly until smooth. Transfer to a bowl and cool in refrigerator for 10 minutes. Remove from refrigerator and stir slowly until smooth and glossy. Makes 3 1/2 cups.

Ingredients

- 2 CUPS HEAVY CREAM
- 16 OUNCES BITTERSWEET CHOCOLATE, 60% CACAO, CHOPPED FINE
- 1 TEASPOON INSTANT COFFEE OR INSTANT ESPRESSO GRANULES

Royal Icing

Combine meringue powder, warm water and powdered sugar in a metal mixing bowl. Beat slowly until stiff peaks form; do not over mix. Icing should not be spongy. Add more water or sugar as needed to reach desired consistency, which will vary depending upon application. Cover with damp cloth if not used right away. This icing hardens and is useful for decorating cakes and other baked goods. Makes 2 cups.

Ingredients

- 5 TABLESPOONS MERINGUE POWDER
- 1/3 CUP WARM WATER
- 4 CUPS POWDERED SUGAR, SIFTED

Fresh Whipped Cream

Place an empty metal mixing bowl and whisk in the freezer to chill for 30 minutes. Sprinkle gelatin into cold water in a bowl and soak or "bloom" for 5 minutes. Remove bowl and tools from freezer and add chilled whipping cream and whip briskly for 5 minutes. While continuing to whip the cream, slowly add the sugar and vanilla extract. Whip cream until it starts to stiffen. Add a small amount of the cream mixture to the prepared gelatin and stir well, then add all of gelatin to the cream. Whip the cream briskly until soft peaks form. Serve immediately or cover and refrigerate for up to 2 days. Makes 4 cups.

Ingredients

- 1 TEASPOON UNFLAVORED GELATIN
- 2 TABLESPOONS COLD WATER
- 2 CUPS CHILLED WHIPPING CREAM
- 2 TABLESPOONS GRANULATED SUGAR
- 1 TABLESPOON VANILLA EXTRACT OR OTHER FLAVORED EXTRACT

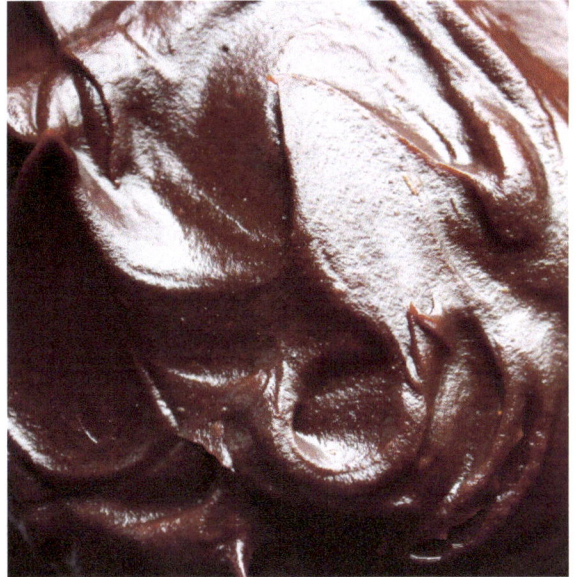

Chocolate Ganache

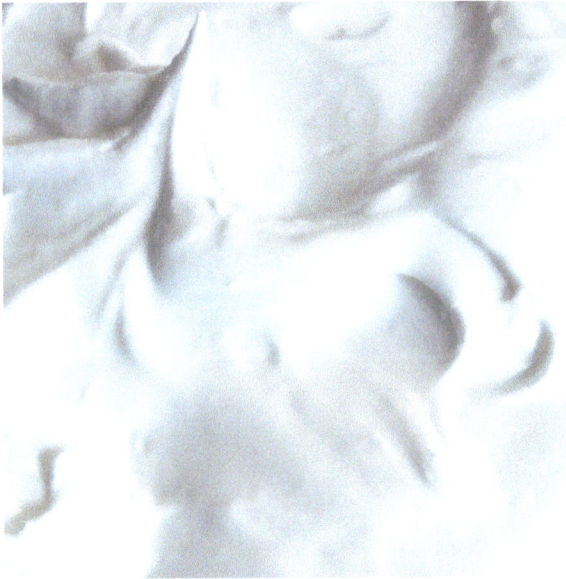

Royal Icing

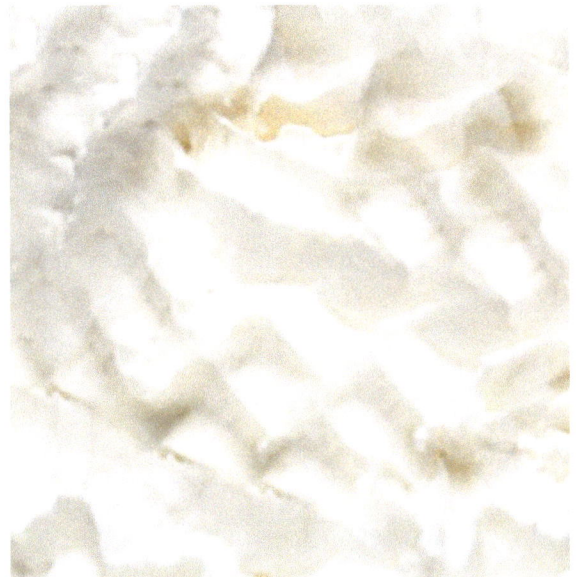

Fresh Whipped Cream

INDEX

Conversions

1/20 ounce	=	penny weight				
1/16 teaspoon	=	dash, what can be picked up between thumb and first two fingers				
1/8 teaspoon	=	pinch				
1/4 teaspoon	=	1 saltspoon				
1 teaspoon	=	1 kitchen spoon	=	1/3 tablespoon		
1 1/2 teaspoons	=	1/2 tablespoon				
3 teaspoons	=	1 tablespoon	=	1/2 ounce		
2 tablespoons	=	1/8 cup	=	1 ounce		
1 jigger	=	1 1/2 oz				
4 tablespoons	=	1/4 cup	=	2 ounces	=	1 goose egg of butter
1 wineglass	=	1/4 cup				
5 tablespoons + 1 teaspoon			=	1/3 cup		
8 tablespoons	=	1/2 cup	=	4 ounces	=	1 gill
12 tablespoons	=	3/4 cup				
1 saucer	=	1 cup				
16 tablespoons	=	1 cup	=	8 ounces	=	1/2 pound
1 tumbler	=	1 cup				
1 cup	=	1 saucer	=	16 tablespoons		
2 cups	=	1 pint	=	32 tablespoons	=	1 pound
8 large eggs	=	1 pound (approximately)				
4 cups	=	2 pints	=	1 quart	=	32 ounces
4 quarts	=	1 gallon	=	128 ounces		
1 peck	=	2 gallons (dry)				
1 firkin of butter	=	9 gallons				
1 hogshead	=	63 gallons				
1 stone	=	14 pounds				

Note: Dry ingredient weights will vary by product and will differ from liquid measurement weights.

Weights for Common Ingredients

1 cup all-purpose flour	5 ounces	142 grams
1 cup granulated (white) sugar	7 ounces	198 grams
1 cup firmly-packed brown sugar	7 ounces	198 grams
1 cup powdered (confectioners') sugar	4 ounces	113 grams
1 cup cocoa powder	3 ounces	85 grams
4 tablespoons butter (1/2 stick)	2 ounces	57 grams
16 tablespoons butter (2 sticks)	8 ounces	228 grams

Oven Temperature Guide (Fahrenheit)

Very slow oven	below 300 degrees
Slow oven	300 degrees
Moderately slow oven	325 degrees
Moderate oven	350 degrees
Moderately hot oven	375 degrees
Quick oven	375 - 400 degrees
Hot oven	400 - 425 degrees
Very hot oven	450 - 475 degrees
Extremely hot oven	500 degrees or more

Vintage Cans

Name	Equivalent
#1	11 ounces
#1 Tall	16-17 ounces
#2	20 ounces
#2 1/2	29 ounces
#2 1/2 Square	31 ounces
#3	32 ounces
#3 Squat	22 ounces
#3 Cylinder	46 ounces
#5	58 ounces
#10	96.5 ounces (also called "Institutional" size)
#300	14-16 ounces
#303	16-17 ounces

Suppliers

Online retailers that sell hard to find spices, baking tools and products:

- ◆ amazon.com
- ◆ ansonmills.com
- ◆ bakeitpretty.com
- ◆ chocosphere.com
- ◆ eBay.com
- ◆ fancyflours.com
- ◆ kingarthurflour.com
- ◆ layerscakeshop.com
- ◆ lorrainescakesupply.com
- ◆ nycake.com
- ◆ thespicehouse.com
- ◆ walmart.com
- ◆ williams-sonoma.com

www.ingramcontent.com/pod-product-compliance
Lightning Source LLC
Chambersburg PA
CBHW042006080426

42733CB00003B/22

* 9 7 8 0 6 1 5 7 8 1 7 6 1 *